A Journey with the Spirit of Life:

STORIES THAT INSPIRE AND ENHANCE HEALING

by John Patrick Gatton

Lifevest Publishing, Inc.
CENTENNIAL, COLORADO

These stories are expressed as though they were told to me. The purpose of these stories and exercises is to stimulate further spiritual imaginings.

J. Patrick Gatton

A Journey with the Spirit of Life
is written by John Patrick Gatton
Copyright 2008 © John Patrick Gatton

Published and Printed by:
Lifevest Publishing
4901 E. Dry Creek Rd., #170
Centennial, CO 80122
www.lifevestpublishing.com

Printed in the United States of America

I.S.B.N. 1-59879-516-3

This book is dedicated
to all our ancestors
who became followers of Jesus
and brought forth the powerful
stories that shaped
our own Christian beliefs.

These are the beliefs that affect
our spiritual, mental, emotional,
and physical health.

They are also powerful influences
on our behavior.

Purpose

Use the stories in this book to saturate your mind with positive images. Doing so will help you to personally feel the powerful effects of positive stories in our lives.

Doing the exercises will additionally expand your imagination, creating positive images and thoughts. These inspiring images and thoughts influence our physical, mental, emotional, and spiritual well-being.

Some stories will seem beyond your imagination. Come back to them, read them again, and accept them as imagination or visualization expanding experiences.

These stories are rich with healing images and thoughts. Enhance your life-journey. Allow these confidence-building stories, thoughts, and images to transport you to new and happier life-experiences.

The Power of a Story and its Telling

Storytelling is about how we think. It is about how we want to think. Storytelling captivates our thinking, enraptures our minds, creates visions, and engages our senses. Within a story, we hear the beat-beat of the marching drums, the sounding of the bugle's awakening call or even the calming voice of an angel reinterpreting the intent of nature.

A well-told story fulfills one's desire to become a believer. It fastens in one's thoughts and confirms progress. It creates the thinking that is unique to men and women. Positive spiritual stories refresh individuals and transport them to a deeper understanding of the Being of Higher Power; the one who is a bountiful provider, and who is Perfect Love.

Stories weave the fibers of our lives into the fabric of our histories. Stories create the directional signs leading us to events that fulfill our need to live life well. Saturating our minds with positive stories causes us to seek, create, perceive, and recognize positive events in our lives. Refreshing ourselves with upbeat images and thoughts becomes the reason we seek and find people and events fostering the enhancement of our own well-being.

Positive stories enable us to set new goals, overcome resistance to change, and stay the course of enhancing our lives. Such stories promote healthy habits and foster success, control, happiness, joy, and the recognition of achievement. As we tell positive stories, we enhance the lives of our family, our friends, and those we are responsible to coach, mentor and encourage.

Some stories in this book should be revisited, as one would revisit a scene that captures your attention. At first reading of a story, deeper meanings go unnoticed just as the first look at a lovely scene leaves important details unnoticed. To grasp the detail of a flower's construction, one must return with more focused attention. So it is with many stories written to ignite the imagination.

BOOK ONE:

The Way of the Cross -
An Example of Perfect Love

Stories and Spiritual Exercises

The Way of the Cross - an Example of Perfect Love

Stories and Spiritual Exercises

Index

Stories written as though they had been told to me.

*In the stories, and the associated exercises,
about the "Way of the Cross"
it is important to find the message of perfect love
that exists within the story or exercise.*

Why I accepted the Way of the Cross

The way became clear to me when I was readying for the Eucharistic Supper. I knew I would make the sacrifice necessary to show the difference between the current bad choices and the Way of Goodness.

I turned to my friends to tell them I would accept the will of the Father. They had to know so they could later recall my words and believe in my veracity. The course was set. As always, it was my choice to accept or choose another path. As a man, I wanted no part of the way to the crucifixion. I cried out to be relieved from the terrible pain and the process of rejection inflicted by this way of dying. However, I had to consider my purpose.

The world's thinking had gone awry. Masses of people had chosen materialism, punishment, war, enslavement, and ritual that meant nothing. Yet they could not comprehend their own lacking of love, their own misconceptions. They could not know the evilness of the ways they pursued, thereby degrading the ways of people from one generation to another.

I accepted the Way of the Cross to transform their perceptions and to point to the error of the path they had chosen. The leaders of the day rejected me and rejected the truth within my works. Therefore, they must rid this world of me. I, the New Way, presented a threat to their path and the direction they perpetuated.

They could not perceive me as a contributor to necessary changes. They could only perceive me as a threat. Since they thought me to be only mortal, they could not accept the possibility that I was the leader of new thinking, a new covenant. They could not allow my good works to continue. I threatened their positions and rituals they believed to be the truth.

I had to choose to allow an apparent win. Evilness would be given its time, the moment in time in which the temple was destroyed. They would not decide to follow the Father's way without a major event proving their direction wrong. Only by the act of resurrection could the people of God be convinced. In accepting the horrible process of the Way of the Cross - as established by leaders of that day, I would show the evilness of their way. This evil way that was so deeply patterned in their minds. By displaying perfect love while accepting this way of indignity, and ever-increasing pain, I would come to the victory that would change the direction of thought in this world. In my hour of choice, I thought of you.

In the greatest of pain, I was to show compassion. Within the ultimate rejection, I was to show forgiveness. In the total wreckage of my body, I was to show tenderness and love. Those who desired to follow me would easily discern this show of compassion and love amid evilness and hate.

I was to suffer at the will of evil so that I might display the tender love of the Father. I was to absorb the hate of evil and speak of salvation; I was to forgive the unforgivable; I was to live - in this terrible dying process - an example of total love. I was to show you the way, even in the most horrible of circumstances.

When I thought of your ancestors who would live following me, when I thought of you and your struggle in life's events, and when I fully realized the need for each following generation for the light and for refreshment, I accepted the Way of the Cross. For those who preceded you, and for the children of all generations, I accepted the way inflicted upon me.

I wanted you to know what love is. I wanted to provide an example that could not be ignored. I extended myself. I wanted to be with you, and so I accepted the cross. I chose for you. Now I recognize and feel joy each time you choose My Way, My Truth, and My Life.

Spiritual exercise:

Sit or lie in your favorite place. Relax. Take in three deep breaths.

Close your eyes. Count back from five down to zero. Each number will take you deeper into relaxation. At three, you will feel more relaxed. When you get to zero you will feel the tension leaving your body.

Stay still for a moment and let go of all tension.

Visualize or imagine being with Jesus as He is gaining an understanding of the purpose of submitting to the Way of the Cross. Imagine now, Jesus realizing that every person in all history, past, present and future will have their fortunes dramatically changed because of His example.

Imagine your feelings as you realize He is making this journey for every person. This means your life and eternal well-being are purposes of His journey. You are important enough for Him to make the choice, and to make the journey of the Way of the Cross.

The Feeling of Abandonment

I am human, you know. It was difficult to let go. Nature said, hold on, but all my friends were gone, except for a few who followed me here. All others stayed away.

My suffering started at around eight in the evening. I knew each moment would be worse until I was on that hill. I came for a purpose. The time remaining was short. Of my works, they made sport.

The feeling began as my brothers slept while I wept in the garden. This feeling was reignited when Judas ran to the authorities of man and started My Way of that beginning day of suffering. I felt abandoned when they put me on trial. I heard Peter say his own denial.

I felt denial, deep and true. Most of my thoughts were about the ancestors of you. If my journey were in vain, they would be lost within their empty behavior.

When they flogged me, I was unable to bear the pain of the wounds. I knew there was no hope and there would be more shocking pain. I looked for kindness but they had shut the door. They spit on me. It felt like acid rain.

After the scourging, they pushed thorns into my head. No mercy was shown. I was alone. I am human, you know. To human feelings, I let go. They slammed the wood onto my open wounds and told me to walk through the city. Only three took pity.

Mentally, I reacted to the severity of the pain, especially when the spit felt like acid rain. I could feel it enter each open vein.

When Veronica gave me the cloth to wipe away the sweat, I felt as though she had given the most love I could get. I felt sane again, and relieved of pain. I painted a portrait that would be a reminder of why I felt abandonment.

Each fall to my knees was more horrible than the last. Into more pain, I would be cast. Then it came - they raised the cross. To describe the pain, even I am at a loss. Through my pain, my mother I could see. I did not know whether to cry, "Please don't watch," or ask her to stay to the end of the day.

Spiritual exercise:

Sit or lie in your favorite place. Relax. Take in three deep breaths.

Close your eyes. Count back from five down to zero. Each number will take you deeper into relaxation. At three, you will feel more relaxed. When you get to zero you will feel the tension leaving your body.

Stay still for a moment and let go of all tension.

Visualize or imagine being with Jesus with your hand on the cloth with Veronica as she hands it to Jesus. Imagine the experience of the light in His eyes as He perceives the kindness of this act.

Imagine the value of this act of kindness to Jesus, as He felt overwhelmed by its meaning, so overwhelmed that He created an image of His face for history.

Imagine being a part of this act of kindness that moved Jesus to create His image on the cloth.

t was the moment for me to speak, to say something to let the world know my thoughts. Then, I saw my mother. Even through my own suffering, her grief was apparent. Knowing that her grief was for my own suffering, I wanted to comfort her.

Looking through my own suffering on the wood, I knew she was present to bring the comfort she could. I thought of her loneliness yet to come as a widow and mother of a crucified son.

She did not know her loss would be brief. To her, the moment was the beginning of a lifetime of missing her son and remembering this horrible occasion. To her, I knew, this would be another lifetime begun in agony and trauma.

I could not repeat my message of resurrection. I had no energy to tell the story of glorification. I had too little stability of emotion to be of extended value to her.

So I simply commended her to be the mother of a new son. And to him, I extended the invitation to care for my mother.

The messages were simple but I knew their effects would be lasting. I knew the reactions of those who had lost a child or a friend. I knew her need to have someone to love and care for.

And so I did the best I could in the condition of low energy and high pain.

I commended my mother to a friend. To my friend, I gave my mother. What more could I do? This act was the only option I had to show my concern for those who came with me on this journey of agony, this journey of showing perfect love.

Spiritual exercise:

Sit or lie in your favorite place. Relax. Take in three deep breaths.

Close your eyes. Count back from five down to zero. Each number will take you deeper into relaxation. At three, you will feel more relaxed. When you get to zero you will feel the tension leaving your body.

Stay still for a moment and let go of all tension. Visualize or imagine being with Mary at the cross and hearing the words of Jesus as he gives her the gift of another son. Imagine the infinite love and kindness existing within Jesus enabling Him to make this gift, even within the pain afflicting His body.

Let the love and kindness that flowed to Mary now flow to you. Accept it. Say, "Thanks."

A Believer

You cannot imagine the shock of hearing so much insult - and then the pleasure of hearing from a believer. The experience on the cross made me especially alert to words said in my defense and words said to help another person understand me.

Imagine my being on the cross - being berated by one who is also suffering, even as I suffered. Imagine the pain of being scorned by a person who is dying with you.

Imagine having left so many friends and having felt all of the cruelty, then being given one more blow from one visiting his own last hours in terrible agony.

Imagine the insult added to the immense pain penetrating my mind from every nerve, then imagine the joy of hearing a word from a believer, a friend, one concerned for me. Imagine the exquisite pleasure of words spoken in defense of me, for me, to refresh me.

Imagine a person I had not known, within in his own agony, saying a word of belief about the value of my life. Imagine the tremendous relief to my mind in its absorption of those kind words.

"What was it like?" you ask.

It was like rain in the desert
It was like mother in darkness
It was like oil on withered skin
It was like food in a hungry time
It was like love in a valley of hate
It was like salt in a tasteless world
It was like mercy in a raping crowd
It was like color seen by blind eyes
It was like release from intense anxiety

It was like manna after severe starvation
It was like a stabilizer in emotional distress
It was like an ocean of love to an abused child
It was like a kindness within a sickened crowd
It was like marvelous wine that briefly intoxicates
It was like a loving word from an estranged brother
It was like reassurance in a distorted sense of loss
It was like having a friend reach out and abate a loss
It was like homespun honey to a body longing for sweetness
It was like a soothing thought floating through a distressed mind

And so, my response was joyful and complete. I could do no less for this good man than he had done for me. I made him a promise that I would fulfill when our agony was finished upon this hill. I could give him no less than he gave to me. Within this day, he would know ecstasy.

Spiritual exercise:

Sit or lie in your favorite place. Relax. Take in three deep breaths.

Close your eyes. Count back from five down to zero. Each number will take you deeper into relaxation. At three, you will feel more relaxed. When you get to zero you will feel the tension leaving your body. Open your eyes.

Stay still for a moment and let go of all tension.
Read and allow your mind to think about each of the above phrases that begins with "It was like ..."

Let yourself realize how important the words of the Good Thief were to Jesus; and the result that came to the Good Thief. Let yourself realize and accept the importance of your own appreciation of Jesus.

Let yourself realize and accept how important your own acts of kindness are to Jesus.

The Thirsting

To thirst beyond the experience of any ordinary circumstance is a horror felt by only a few within all sufferings in the world.

During my time of suffering -

I had fainted in agony
I had been bitterly cold
I had felt my bones pierced
I had been tempted to give up
I had split my knees open in falls
I had suffered the pain of the whip
I had been blinded by my own blood
I had been bitterly sick to my stomach
I had awakened to fright filled moments

Now, I was thirsty to the marrow of my bones. It was a time when all other pain seemed to cease in comparison. I wanted each cell to be refreshed. Every cell called for water, for refreshment.

The agony of the thirst for life-giving fluid was worse than the agony of the nails. Finally, I could no longer tolerate the suffering. I had to request help. I needed compassion, a compassionate act. I pleaded, "I thirst."

At this time the sacrifice was near completion. But I had to endure one more insult, one more infliction of disgust upon me. I was given brine to add to the horror of the thirst. This thirst made me aware of each cell of my body.

I could not rid myself of this brine placed in my mouth. It added to my overwhelming dehydration. Once again, I was brought to realize the breadth and depth of sin, the error of man's thinking, which was the cause of my suffering.

Later, when I was refreshed in spirit and in resurrection, I carried the memory of that thirst. Even now, I carry this memory. This memory is the reason I promise those who provide drink to the thirsty and food to the hungry shall dwell with me. When I said, "I thirst," each cell registered that moment's memory.

When one of mine feels similar pain and is assisted by my follower, I promise to reward the act with pleasantness more penetrating than a soaking, sweet rain.

Spiritual exercise:

Sit or lie in your favorite place. Relax. Take in three deep breaths.

Close your eyes. Count back from five down to zero. Each number will take you deeper into relaxation. At three, you will feel more relaxed. When you get to zero you will feel the tension leaving your body.

Stay still for a moment and let go of all tension.
Visualize or imagine bringing a glass of water to a person who is thirsty. This person could be doing any of the following:

> Lying in a hospital bed
> Planting flowers
> Running in a marathon
> Caring for a child
> Caring for a sick person
> Dizzy from the heat of the day

> _____

> _____

Consider how Jesus would view your act of kindness based on this story about His thirsting.

I was at the end of any source of living and ability to resist the temptation to give up. At this moment, I felt abandoned with too little energy to put forth one positive thought. I was flooded with doubt. "Father," I cried, "Why have you forsaken me?" In memory of this moment, I know of your own lack of strength. In your own time of giving up, I am reminded of my own experience.

When you say you can no longer bear the pain, I remember the reality that was my own. Within this memory, I feel compassion for you. In your own giving over to the pain of the trial, I intercede with the Father to hear your cry.

Your own personal moments of giving-up create occasions for positive actions. It is within these times that the Father fills you with His own Spirit. When you are at your least, He fills you with Himself, just as He did for me.

I tell you this so you may understand my personal empathy has come from my own agony. Could I forget the memory that dwells in my cells?

Spiritual exercise:

Sit or lie in your favorite place. Relax. Take in three deep breaths. Close your eyes. Count back from five down to zero. Each number will take you deeper into relaxation. At three, you will feel more relaxed. When you get to zero you will feel the tension leaving your body. Stay still for a moment and let go of all tension. Let the tension flow out of your body.

Visualize or imagine standing face-to-face with Jesus. Say to Jesus, "I trust in You, I give myself over to You. Let your strength become mine that I may find within myself a solution to this problem."

Let yourself realize that Jesus has experienced what you are feeling.

Imagine His Divine light flowing through you. Allow this light to flow to where it is needed within you. Let this light help you find the right solution within yourself.

The Spirit

Within the closing of my eyes, I was filled with the Spirit. Finally, I could release from this agony. There were no more temptations to endure. Again, I was filled with Grace.

I knew I had triumphed. I knew now that I must bear no more of this excruciating trial. In every cell, every vibration within me, I could feel now the peace of the Father. There was nothing left for me to fulfill. There was no reason to hold out, to fight against, to restrain, and no need to try. I was at peace. I was ready for the transition.

Though exhausted to the last ounce of energy, I wanted to give you one last signal of my love. I could not think, for there was no energy remaining. I could have only a desire to say a last word for you.

Today, one can look back upon those words and draw many meanings from them. However, at the time, I could only do what was natural. Once again I commended myself and my journey to His Will - His judgment.

I could do nothing more than a habitual, and natural, act. I could only follow the habit developed in my life experiences. I could only exclaim an automatic response, "Father, into Your hands I commend my Spirit."

How often I had said those words in the trials I faced as Son of Man. How often I relied on His wisdom to move me through temptation that was only partly apparent to me. How often He had guided me in discerning right choices from wrong. I had become accustomed to relying on His judgment known through my own inner voice.

It was natural for me to turn my life over to Him. Habitual, natural, and well rewarded, was this act of mine. Therefore, at the ending of this journey, it was a natural response for me to utter the phrase signaling both Him and you that I am His son.

By imitating this act of mine in your own life, you will come to understand I gave all over to Him. I recommend you do the same.

For, as I have exampled, I am.

As I am, I am glorified.

In my glory, I invite you to practice turning always to Him. Always shift the weight of discernment to Him. In this practice, you will find peace. It will become natural for you to turn to Him, even in your final release.

Spiritual exercise:

Sit or lie in your favorite place. Relax. Take in three deep breaths.

Close your eyes. Count back from five down to zero. Each number will take you deeper into relaxation. At three, you will feel more relaxed. When you get to zero you will feel the tension leaving your body. Stay still for a moment and let go of all tension. Let the tension flow out of your body.

Handwrite the following: "As my goal, Father, I commend myself to You, to Your will, and to Your judgment. My goal is to live in full unity with You. I will achieve this goal through, with, and in unity with Jesus and the Holy Spirit."

Each time you go to bed for a night's rest, say the following just as you are preparing to sleep, "As my goal, Father, I commend myself to you; to your will; to your judgment. My goal is to live in full unity with you. I will achieve this goal through, with, and in unity with Jesus and the Holy Spirit."

In My Arms, His Body Lies

As might be told by Mary, mother of Jesus.

We brought Him down from the cross. My emotions were rattled and mixed. I knew it would be a long time before they healed again.

He had finished with suffering and yet He was gone from me. I was relieved at the release of His agony, yet my emotions rolled in full dimension within each second.

My body was still hurting from the identification with His pain. Now, I was grieving the loss of Him. Already, I missed Him. We were wonderful friends. I could hear myself wailing. I could feel myself rocking. I could feel my nerves deadening.

I realized then, I had lifted my son's body onto my lap and I was full of desire to feed Him nourishment that would revive Him. I was powerless and could only respond to the enormous swing of my emotions.

Remember this in your devotions, I grieved and felt the human outcry as anyone does when such an event slams into one's life. I could only release Him when my friends insisted. My time of confusion began.

Spiritual exercise:

Sit or lie in your favorite place. Relax. Take in three deep breaths. Close your eyes. Count back from five down to zero. Each number will take you deeper into relaxation. At three, you will feel more relaxed. When you get to zero you will feel the tension leaving your body. Stay still for a moment and let go of all tension. Let the tension flow out of your body.

Visualize or imagine you are present at the foot of the cross and comforting Mary, mother of Jesus. Know that her role soon will be to tell the stories of the life of Jesus. These stories will be important to all followers of Jesus.

Tell Mary, "We are with you. We need you now. We need to know of His life, His purpose."

Resurrection

My soul released, I was at peace.

I had an important task to complete quite soon
to bring souls to a heavenly room
where the Father could say, "This is your day!"

Then it was time to be reunited with my humanness
and there I stood ready to leave through the opened door,
My body was healed.

First to mother to say I am here.
She could see my joy.
Joy did I say?
I looked around and as I smiled
I think all of heaven literally went wild!

I was resurrected!
I had finished the work, now I was returned to glory.

I was so happy for what I had done for my Father.
I had done it for Him and you and yours.
It was accomplished.

I was so happy, so exalted - you see
I could hear every voice that was singing for me.
I heard every word.
I heard from each who said a word or phrase to bless my head.

Imagine the happiness of having friends celebrate your deeds!
That's how I felt! I had planted the seeds!

I heard every voice.
I knew you would add yours when your time came on Earth.
Your love makes me happy.

MARY – *The Joy of His Easter Visit*

You are the Son!
You are the one whom the Father desired for us.

Oh, I knew, however, it was so hard to stay and
believe fully on Saturday.

Now that I am reassured, let me cry with joy.
I am happy to see you, my boy!

My boy. Oh, I am relieved, for you and all who believed.

Thank you for coming.
I know you are here because our relationship is ever so dear.

Oh, my son, you are the one who saved us all!
Let me touch you now.
Let me caress your face.
Let me see the healed wounds.
Let me stroke your hair.

Oh, son, what is that essence you wear?
It smells so heavenly, from where can it be?
Is it the Father's blessing that let you return to me?

Oh, son hold me close.
Let me put my arms 'round.
Talk to me now.
Let me hear your sound.

Oh, my son, my fear for you is gone.
The horror I felt is past.
Joy, the peaceful confirmation that we were right
has captured my soul.
I will hold tightly to this feeling of peace.
Joy itself - I will caress.

Let us rejoice together.

The Disciples realized little of The Way when I left them. Their own doubtful thoughts strongly mixed with the truth of the Word. Through the Spirit they were given:

The gift of retention
The gift of conviction
The gift of persuasion
The gift of discernment
The gift of early believers
The gift of openness to hear
The gift of right interpretation
The gift of humor within frustration
The gift of a partially receptive nation
The gift of learning through participation

They shared their gifts. As they shared, the community strengthened. This strength made easier the spread of the Word of God.

Spiritual Exercise:

Sit or lie in your favorite place. Relax. Take in three deep breaths. Close your eyes. Count back from five down to zero. Each number will take you deeper into relaxation. At three, you will feel more relaxed. When you get to zero you will feel the tension leaving your body. Stay still for a moment and let go of all tension. Let the tension flow out of your body.

Visualize or imagine scenes in the life of Jesus, the Christ, as you read from the New Testament. When you visualize or imagine scenes based on the stories in the New Testament, let yourself see the details of the scene. Imagine details including - the desert, the mountain, the sand, the hot sun, the disciples gathered around

Jesus, the women who provide housing and food and encourage others to know Jesus, the whispering doubters, healing, the woman touching His cloak, the Leper's restored health, the crowd that is being fed from a loaf and fishes, the child who meets Jesus for the first time, the face of the mother whose child Jesus resurrected.

Corpus Christi, Body of Christ

Deep in the recess of the heart is the meaning of the name, Corpus Christi. The name reveals more than the mind initially comprehends. Do you understand yet? It is you upon whom the extent and depth of my life in this community depends.

Who am I, then, without you? Less, says the poet, however, many have to contemplate a lifetime to know it. You, my friend, are one upon whom I depend.

Your choice of being here, among my own, makes my heart ring with cheer. Know you that I depend on you? It is you whom I love. Do you know that you, personally, add to my splendor and it is you who makes more of the Body of Christ?

Through your own personal touch you are a part of the core, the homeostasis. My friend, your integration with the community means so much. I am stabilized in this community because of you and the beliefs you keep in your embraces. With you the goodness of the Body of Christ is expanded. With your contributions, those of others are multiplied.

The Body of Christ! Think of this, you are a contributing member! Realize this, my friend, when you enter a church, when you entertain a friend, when you reach to help, when you pay so another may enjoy, when you pray, and when you intercede, you are contributing to the community which is the Body of Christ.

Written for the dedication of the new Corpus Christi parish church, Chatham NJ 1990

Spiritual exercise:

Sit or lie in your favorite place. Relax. Take in three deep breaths. Close your eyes. Count back from five down to zero. Each number will take you deeper into relaxation. At three, you will feel more relaxed. When you get to zero you will feel the tension leaving your body. Stay still for a moment and let go of all tension. Let the tension flow out of your body.

Visualize or imagine being with a person who is in need. As you talk with this person and offer help, the kindness of Jesus is flowing through you in the form of warming, healing light. Visualize or imagine this same light pouring through you to each person with whom you come into contact. Allow the healing light of Jesus to flow to the person through you, helping to achieve positive personal goals.

BOOK TWO:

Peter, the Rock
Possibilities

Stories About Saint Peter's
Spiritual development
With Spiritual exercises
to encourage meditation

Possibilities

Definition of a possibility:

A possibility is what could happen if we changed perceived conditions, eliminated restrictions, and enlarged our expectations.

Background

The traditional stories told about Peter, the Rock, no doubt contain truths about his character. However, he became the leader of one of the most significant religions on earth. How did this fisherman evolve into a most significant leader whose thinking influences many millions of people in a yet untold number of generations?

The stories contained in this collection may help broaden the view of the greatness of this man and stimulate additional imaginative stories about him. It would be good to read hundreds of stories about the changes Peter experienced in his earthly life. Stories that describe his progress while developing as a leader within the spiritual guidance of Jesus would be welcomed. These stories put forth some imaginings about how Peter was <u>gifted</u> to meet the challenges of leading persistent human thought through dramatic changes.

Peter provided the necessary leadership to form a new way of thinking while preserving the goodness contained in ancient history.

Note about the author's belief: though the experiences were Peter's to live, Jesus would have orchestrated them in unity with the Holy Spirit. These poetic stories are expressed as though they were told to me.

J. Patrick Gatton

Possibilities

Index

Stories written as though they had been told to me.

Perfecting

Life's journey is not about being perfect but about perfecting.

Perfecting is a process beginning with knowledge that stimulates the mind, opening it to other ideas. Selecting fresh ideas as working assumptions follows the acceptance of those ideas.

Desire follows acceptance of new ideas. Desire is essential to forming the image of what one wants to be. With the new idea or image in place, the individual selects the route and the methods of changing behavior.

Then, comes the willing. To change, one must redirect thoughts, words, actions, and responses. One must let go of the habitual thinking and accept new ways of living and thinking.

In each letting go and each accepting, the will is active until old ways are less attractive and new experiences are preferred.

When you review my life, remember my imperfections (for they too are examples), however, dwell on the process of my development.

My story of perfecting did not end on the inverted cross, but that is another story.

Seeing in a Distance

From atop the mountain peak he could see a distance. The unimpaired line of sight took his thoughts to the creator of all terrain and space.

Then, given the gift to count the stars, he recognized infinity.

When he came to a trillion, he could no longer keep record and yet more than those already counted blinked beyond his discerning view.

In this experience he learned that the end did not exist in the stars but lay in his own limited expectations, faculties, and perceived situations.

This learning created new possibilities.

Spiritual exercise:

Sit or lie in your favorite place. Relax. Take in three deep breaths.

Close your eyes. Count back from five down to zero. Each number will take you deeper into relaxation. At three, you will feel more relaxed. When you get to zero you will feel the tension leaving your body.

Stay still for a moment and let go of all tension.

**Handwrite the following: "I give permission for the release of all thoughts that restrict me from seeking new possibilities in my relationship with Jesus. I open myself to new ways to know and follow Jesus."

**Each evening as you are going to sleep, read the above statement. This exercise sets the permission and the goal into your subconscious mind.

** This procedure is put forth by Dr. John Kappas in his process titled "Mental Bank." Dr. Kappas was the founder of Hypnosis Motivation Institute. www.hypnosis.edu

Life is Different

My life with the Savior is now different than it was in my earthly life.

He has infused me, along with many others, with all knowledge.

No longer do I stand before Him with simple human knowledge.

When He speaks, I know of His reference and I understand His intent.

His plan is clear to me. I am confident in this understanding; this clarity.

I am anxious to do His will without doubt and lacking anxiety.

I need only to make effortless effort to fulfill His wish. Effort being important, I must will to help. In my own willing and participation in His life, He is fully with me. He anticipates, and fulfills my desires. This makes my soul resonate to His call for any help at all.

I live peacefully but always anticipating His call. So, open yourself to Him that He may call me to serve you.

Spiritual exercise:

Sit or lie in your favorite place. Relax. Take in three deep breaths.

Close your eyes. Count back from five down to zero. Each number will take you deeper into relaxation. At three, you will feel more relaxed. When you get to zero you will feel the tension leaving your body.

Stay still for a moment and let go of all tension.

Now visualize or imagine being with Jesus and saying to Him something like the following, "I will read of your good acts in the New Testament. I will gain an understanding of what those good acts mean to me. I open myself to imitate those acts in my own life. I ask for your help in my using your example to pattern my own actions."

Friends of All Generations

With me, in this spiritual life, are friends from all generations. They also love the Lord and are in accord with the vibrations of the energies of creation.

Some of these folks I knew in earth-life. However, my own limited ability to perceive the completeness and beauty of their souls restricted my experience of them.

What does it mean to have a sublime friend? It is a bit of ecstasy in itself to have a friend whose soul is attuned to the creation energies. A soul that resonates to nature's voice is a marvelous companion. Observing ecstasy and being ecstatic in the same instant creates sublime after-effects.

In earthly years, I knew ecstasy. In all that has come after, I know the sublime.

Within your soul, I detect the tendency to desire to know the presence of God. Because you want to know this presence, I am inclined to be with you. Being with you, my own being resonates in the joy of the universe.

Spiritual exercise:

Sit or lie in your favorite place. Relax. Take in three deep breaths.

Close your eyes. Count back from five down to zero. Each number will take you deeper into relaxation. At three, you will feel more relaxed. When you get to zero you will feel the tension leaving your body.

Stay still for a moment and let go of all tension.

Visualize or imagine seeing Peter, the spiritual leader of the initial Christian Movement. As you move close to Peter, allow yourself to imagine how his face brightens as he sees you. Know that a cause of Peter's joy in seeing you is your desire to be with God. Your desire brings delight to him because he lived and died for the acceptance of Jesus, the Christ in our lives.

An Ordinary Man

I was a fisherman both impetuous and headstrong. I was never concerned about leading other people until He gifted me to be a leader.

I lived with human frailties never thinking these frailties would be of concern to others. Little did I know that even those frailties would become examples for folks of all times.

Jesus makes strong those who carry weaknesses and frailties. Many of us do live with weaknesses.

He seasoned me and helped me develop as a leader while acknowledging that my own frailties would become well known in the world. I, being an ordinary man, became the example of one chosen and put well into service in the Lord's work.

Spiritual exercise:

Sit or lie in your favorite place. Relax. Take in three deep breaths.

Close your eyes. Count back from five down to zero. Each number will take you deeper into relaxation. At three, you will feel more relaxed. When you get to zero you will feel the tension leaving your body.

Stay still for a moment and let go of all tension.

Visualize or imagine sitting at a table having a meal with Peter. Listen to the words he speaks about our human frailties and how Jesus accepts us with those frailties, those weaknesses. Listen also to the words Peter says about our being children of God. As God's children we have talents, capabilities and responsibilities.

Review the talents you have been given. Acknowledge your own skills and desires to serve. Let yourself realize that, with the help of Jesus, you can contribute through your own efforts.

Let yourself imagine how Peter made the transition from being a simple man to being a profound spiritual leader. Imagine additional events he experienced with Jesus as his guide.

Twelve of us were the leaders and the symbol of a new nation. We were simple in our experience as leaders. We were not yet infused with appropriate knowledge to perform the tasks required to example The Way of Jesus.

We followed without courage. We wandered in bewilderment.

We believed because we experienced His abilities. His charismatic attraction fascinated us. Who could leave a man of such healing powers?

We were simple in our common knowledge. Our insights developed in simple terms. Our steadfastness in love was untested. We had no planned direction for following the command to teach and no means to create one.

We were fascinated, mated with an irresistible force.

We walked behind, then, we were given the power to heal. We learned that His power could be extended. However, without Him, the sense of the gift was diminished.

We were men of little spiritual stability having to wait for a mystic and ecstatic experience to find perseverance in our belief.

Spiritual exercise:

Sit or lie in your favorite place. Relax. Take in three deep breaths.

Close your eyes. Count back from five down to zero. Each number will take you deeper into relaxation. At three, you will feel more relaxed. When you get to zero you will feel the tension leaving your body.

Stay still for a moment and let go of all tension.

Visualize or imagine the Disciples discovering that they had been given the power to heal others. Imagine their surprise when a crippled person was able to walk simply because the Disciple said, "Get up, and walk."

Let yourself realize that these Disciples, and all who followed them were human and they had to desire to be with Jesus. They willed to act as He acted, and took the action that seemed beyond their capabilities. They had to believe The Word and had to act on their beliefs.

Because of their humanity, the Disciples had to listen to The Word, will to act, experience the results of their actions, and adjust to the fact that, with Jesus, they were meeting a potential they had not even dared dream about.

Now, let yourself realize that, within the direction of Jesus, you have much more potential to contribute and make a difference that makes a difference. One reason is that Jesus brings infinite resources to help you achieve your good goals.

Expectations

We find great things through expecting to find them.

We expected great things of Jesus. John the Baptist set our perceptions - "Follow-Him," said John.

He looked like an ordinary man, this Jesus. Nevertheless, He had innate inner peace and unwavering confidence. He healed knowing it was real and permanent.

He spoke from the pages of history telling stories and interpreting them into modern life. He was confident in His abilities, using His abilities to help those who requested it.

He was humble and magnanimous in His love for men and women. He knew more of people than they knew of themselves and healed them because they believed. These healings told much of Him.

All who came were healed according to His will. He knew the quality of His healing and dispensed it with compassion, without self-absorption.

He appreciated a word of thanksgiving, but did not require it. He healed to show love and to indicate who He was. He gave these healings as examples to be remembered and used in our own lives.

Spiritual exercise:

Sit or lie in your favorite place. Relax. Take in three deep breaths.

Close your eyes. Count back from five down to zero. Each number will take you deeper into relaxation. At three, you will feel more relaxed. When you get to zero you will feel the tension leaving your body. Stay still for a moment and let go of all tension.

Visualize or imagine meeting Jesus with His followers in a place where they have gathered to rest. Walk up to Jesus and say, "Jesus, I need your help." Listen for His reply.

He may say, "The help you need has been given." He may say, "Go to the Priest and volunteer to help others. As you help others, the help you need is already given." He may say, "Follow me, let go of what binds you and do as I do." He may say, "Return to your family and celebrate life with them."

The Desire to Serve

Knowing Him created my own desire to serve Him.

I was charmed by His confidence, calmness, healings, teaching, love.

Experiencing the confidence and acts of Jesus did cause fear in some people. Some ran from His sight. However, knowing His motive to heal, I moved close to Him.

As He healed us, He became more attracting to us. In this attraction, I desired to become active in His ministry. My desire to heal, give witness, and reach out to help others increased in each day's dawning. I wanted to function with Him and within His infinite love.

Now, as you are attracted to Jesus, be aware that there are other options you could select. Be grateful that love is continually your selection for even love is a gift.

Spiritual exercise:

Sit or lie in your favorite place. Relax. Take in three deep breaths.

Close your eyes. Count back from five down to zero. Each number will take you deeper into relaxation. At three, you will feel more relaxed. When you get to zero you will feel the tension leaving your body.

Stay still for a moment and let go of all tension. Visualize or imagine being near Jesus and observing that His presence is immensely attracting. Let yourself discover the elements of His being that are so attracting you must move closer to Him. His inner peace draws you into itself. The light He emits is healing. His eyes are bright with acceptance of you. His hands beckon you to move to Him. His stance is relaxed and confident. He is Perfect Love that causes ecstasy within you. Each step closer to Him increases your own self confidence.

As you notice more detail, observe the Angels with him. Each Angel motions you forward, closer to His presence.

Searching

We walked many miles from place to place on the Mediterranean's shores while living through many events and searching for our own goals and accomplishments.

We frequently encountered surprise requests. With these requests, we received the gifts of healing and refreshing people in mind, body, and spirit.

As we gained experience as instruments of healing, our frame of reference changed. However, even in our own advancement and acceptance of the surprise, greater surprises occurred.

The journey of conversation,
>   and teaching,
>   and healing,
>   and discussion
>   was never predictable.

We had to trust.

We had to follow The Word, as our minds heard it.

We did not know what test of our confidence would next arise. Each request and each response carried its own surprise.

Spiritual exercise:

Sit or lie in your favorite place. Relax. Take in three deep breaths. Close your eyes. Count back from five down to zero. Each number will take you deeper into relaxation. At three, you will feel more relaxed. When you get to zero you will feel the tension leaving your body. Stay still for a moment and let go of all tension.

Visualize or imagine saying, "Jesus, I want to have more trust in what I can accomplish with and through You." Listen to your inner voice. Remember the response.

Note: Discerning the quality of the message of the "inner voice" is based on predicting or observing the results of taking action based on the content of the message. If the results are positive in their affects on you and others, the quality of the message is good. Becoming proficient in this discernment may require spending some time with a Spiritual Director.

The Wind

The wind upon the sea is under some control, but what controls it? What pressure fabricates the wind?

Two conclusions seem logical. The first is that the wind acts according to law.

The second is that the wind can be moved by God's will. This latter conclusion is supported by the story of Jesus calming the sea.

Since the wind may be moved by will, how are we to view its animation? What is the purpose of the one who wills the vitality of the wind? Certainly, we should ask.

The balance of nature contains the wind. People learn to use it to their advantage.

However, does a wind contain the destinations of people?

As with a sail that catches a proper wind, so it is with each of us. We search for, and recognize, the right wind with which to sail. Then, in happiness, we face the challenges and reap the rewards contained within that same wind's force and direction.

Spiritual Exercise:

In this story, the wind is a metaphor, meaning a force that moves and drives an object in its own journey.

In our lives, the forces that move us are both internal and external. Those forces that move and drive us to good results are positive in nature. Those forces that move and drive us to be less than we should be are negative in nature.

Handwrite the forces you think are moving you to positive results. Those forces include your habits, your thoughts, and your beliefs, your interactions with others, your ethics, and the examples you follow.

I stood near the sea to hear the sounds of nature when suddenly I knew I was attuned to the vibrations of the universe.

I felt within me the vibrations of the moon's core and the effect it has in the water of this sea's shore.

I felt the sun's center rock and heave and in its wake, a universal vibration leave.

I felt Jupiter stir in its circle and cause the vibration of the city's walls.

I felt the wind change as nature spoke its name.

I felt moisture rise to meet its own destiny as rain, simply because Mother Nature thought it should do so.

I felt the movement of the particles of earth touching my feet.

I felt oxygen in my lungs and knew the gift given by the trees.

I knew that I must breathe out that they breathe in.

I knew that they must breathe out that I breathe in.

I was surprised at these insights. This shared knowledge of the universe confirmed me as a part of its energy. This knowledge now keeps me aware of all the gifts we share when we turn to help those in trouble and despair.

Spiritual Exercise:

Either go outside, or visualize or imagine being outside with your feet touching the warm ground.

Take in three deep breaths. Relax.

Set your mental focus on the bottoms of your feet. Let yourself feel the vibrations of the earth. As you feel these vibrations, let them release all negative memories and tensions from your body.

Now let yourself realize that your own body vibrations are synchronized with those of the Mother Earth. Allow yourself to realize that being in concert with Nature and Positive Forces is one way to make you congruent with Nature and its Creator.

Being congruent with the Creator is the source of inner peace.

Unexpected Experiences

What do you think it was like for the Disciples to see the sick healed and the blind cured at their own willing and touch?

What do you think it was like for me to experience events like the following -

> To stand and be in ecstasy
> To walk and have mother earth reverberate to the touch of my feet
> To talk and change the direction of thinking
> To sing and have harps respond
> To eat and drink with God
> To hear the trees weep in happiness at my human touch
> To experience water springing forth under a digging finger
> To create calm where mayhem reigned
> To surge forth with delight at the hearing of the name of Jesus
> To master a language while in an initial conversation
> To lean on a well's wall and have it fill with water
> To mark a place as holy and have a church raised on that place
> To make a mark with one's foot in impenetrable rock
> To mark the beginning of a new belief system

Spiritual Exercise:

Read any event written above. Relax; let your imagination take over. Imagine the shocks to Peter's own systems in these events; and the growth of his character triggered by each of these events.

Celebration of His Birth

Today is significant as the celebration of His birth.

None has known for sure all the reasons for His coming as Son of Man. However, over the millennium I have absorbed some knowledge yet untold.

> We know He came to love.
> We know He came to example.
> We know He came to heal.

He came to example - trust, joy, compassion, feeling, extension of self, the power of positive thought, strength transmitted in words, the holiness of persons, and power through belief.

He came to example - the affects of focused energy, kindness, attention to goodness, miraculous touch, care for the sick, resolution in adversity, and healing light.

He came to example - resurrection, multiplication of loaves, faith in the Father, self-love combined with humility, the source of happiness, and the process of achieving joy.

He came to example - loving light, instantaneous forgiveness, reconciliation, welcoming, identification with the sick of soul, magnificent attractiveness, and irresistible love.

He came to example - forgetfulness in favor of a sinner, life sharing, intense loyalty to the truth, powerful commands based in unequivocal faith, absolute confidence in the Father's promise, resolute tenacity, resilience, acceptance of another's willing, and the warmth of a spiritual call.

He came to example - rightful indignation, useful anger, valued discussion among friends, sensitive response to curiosity, freedom to accept those who are outcasts, confidence in the journeying person, and assurance of the abundance of love.

He came to extend the domain of love.

Spiritual exercise:

Sit or lie in your favorite place. Relax. Take in three deep breaths.

Close your eyes. Count back from five down to zero. Each number will take you deeper into relaxation. At three, you will feel more relaxed. When you get to zero you will feel the tension leaving your body.

Stay still for a moment and let go of all tension.

Visualize or imagine seeing Jesus in the distance and walking up to Him while he greets you as a friend and one for whom He lived on this earth. As you talk with Jesus, let yourself realize that He is your friend and He is Source with the Father and the Holy Spirit.

He is a loyal friend, your Redeemer, and a part of the Source of all life. Allow yourself to be given some understanding of the warmth, inner peace, and confidence that comes just by being in the presence of Jesus.

An Enduring Friend

You and I have bonded our relationship.

You have endeared an enduring friend.

I am with you and call for grace when you arrive in the place of those desiring your presence.

I bring along a heavenly crew that sings, touches, heals, and calls for graces for those showing their faces where you are. When you help others to heal, I am always about, for I enjoy watching the celestial forces give negative thought the rout.

I love you, my friend. Know that I go with you to those you visit. With me, He has sent a rapturous show of friends and light and the concentration of wisdom and insight.

With me, I bring:
An Angel to sing
A harp to play
A keeper of love
A displayer of concern
An ancient one gifted with words
A spirited horse of fiery display
A mule pulling a cart of jeweled light
A crystal magnifier of the light
A tune that heals
A player of bells
A seal of compassion
A turn of emotions
An inspirer of devotions
A stimulator of peace
An angel with the touch of happiness
An echo of laughter from the castle of God
A sizable friend to push the wind
A bit of majesty for each to see
A rose from the garden of love
A key that unlocks spiritual doors

A tonic that soothes the heart
An ointment that saturates cells and replaces the dark
Ancient ones who experienced the same as those of today
A relic of the ancestral line of those who passed along the divine
A jovial story
An improved view of life
A portion of celestial balance
A beam of love from the Father's crown
A diamond of white light given by Jesus
A share of energy given by the universe

All of these I bring when you reach to help and to heal within your community.

Spiritual exercise:

Sit or lie in your favorite place. Relax. Take in three deep breaths.

Close your eyes. Count back from five down to zero. Each number will take you deeper into relaxation. At three, you will feel more relaxed. When you get to zero you will feel the tension leaving your body.

Stay still for a moment and let go of all tension.

Visualize or imagine going to visit a person who is in need. Ask Peter, the Rock, to join you in your visit with this person in need.

Reread the above list and allow yourself to become aware of the good things Peter brings along in this visit. Or, select one of the items listed above and request that Peter share that item with the person who is in need.

Give yourself permission to have full confidence in Peter's assistance. Say, "Thanks."

Feeling somewhat confused and lost, a man began to swirl and cook a briny view of life. As he commenced, he heard a distinct but distant voice asking, "What is your choice?"

The voice was one of commanding presence. There was no option to remain silent.

The man had to answer.

Somehow, he knew the question implied a choice of right or wrong; a choice of peace or a choice of a debilitating song.

Within the moment, he answered in this way, "It is with goodness I want to be. I have seen enough evil; I can only choose goodness."

"You have again come to life," said the voice of light, love, and oneness. This distinct voice was in harmony with all nature, all nations. "Feel, now, the pull of love's magnetism. Resist not the need within you to reach out to others and enhance their view of life's purpose."

"Search and find those needing help to live with the existing conditions. Look for those who need to know that goodness is near and within them. It is they who will make your own mission clear," said the voice of distinction.

Spiritual exercise:

Sit or lie in your favorite place. Relax. Take in three deep breaths. Close your eyes. Count back from five down to zero. Each number will take you deeper into relaxation. At three, you will feel more relaxed. When you get to zero you will feel the tension leaving your body. Stay still for a moment and let go of all tension.

Visualize or imagine being in a quiet place with your eyes closed; hearing the voice of a friend telling you that those in need need you. Those in need may be in a career crisis, may have a disease, may be depressed, may need a simple prayer, may need to spend time with a friend, may need to get some exercise to relieve loneliness, or may simply need a kind word.

Visualize or imagine going to the person in need, chatting and asking what you can do to be of help. Visualize or imagine meeting the person's need.

Reaching to help another person creates inner harmony and healing of self.

Stars strike a pose for God as He wills. The physical arrangement of the stars creates motion in the universe. This motion distributes itself as energy to the beings of the Universe. Primal and sophisticated urges revive for fulfillment in the wake of the energy created by the motion of stars.

Relaxation dawns when quieting energy of a star's motion transfers to living beings. Each day, each move of the stars happens according to His plan. He calculated the effects of all the moves and knows their timing.

Your life is sustained by multiple energies and their synergies. All of these are known, and willed by Source.

Even profound human awareness recognizes only a few of these influences. So stretch your imagination. Ask for insights. Let knowledge pour in. I have requested that you be filled with all knowledge you can accept.

Forget the comments of those who disdain. Honor your own insights. What do you have to lose? Unless, of course, you refuse.

Spiritual exercise:

Sit or lie in your favorite place. Relax. Take in three deep breaths.

Close your eyes. Count back from five down to zero. Each number will take you deeper into relaxation. At three, you will feel more relaxed. When you get to zero you will feel the tension leaving your body.

Stay still for a moment and let go of all tension.

Visualize or imagine you are in a place in the Universe where all knowledge is stored in well-organized libraries. All knowledge is easily accessed and given to anyone who desires to use it for good purposes.

Decide what knowledge you would like to have and use for good purposes. Request the resources needed to acquire the knowledge you need to serve your purpose.

Choose the Door

The house is shaped with a steep roof.

This door opens from either side.

Which side to unlock is your choice.

As you choose, listen to the inner voice.

The house is Jerusalem; the door is your way of life.

The direction in which you choose to open the door will destroy your heart or set it afire.

"What, or whom, do you chose?"

This is always the question within life's decisions.

What, or whom, you chose to desire is clearly the choice.

The will is challenged, though not always fully.

Each selection made is for a bit of the peaceful, or the unruly.

BOOK THREE:

Stages in Heaven

An Imaginary Journey
into Infinite Goodness

Stages in Heaven
An Imaginary Journey into Infinite Goodness

Index

Stories written as though they had been told to me.

Stages in Heaven - Five Writings
An Imaginary Journey
into Infinite Goodness

I have written about Heaven before. Two of the most remembered of those writings are titled, "Imagine" and "Stages in Heaven."

The poem "Imagine" was written March 24, 1985 the day after our daughter, Cynthia Jean Gatton, died in an automobile crash while in college.

The two poems, "Imagine," and "Stages in Heaven," appear before the sequence of five new writings to reinforce the idea that it is possible to imagine Heaven. Many authors have written about hellish experiences; why not write about Heaven and infinite goodness?

Daddy, I am ecstatic. You must write my poem for my friends.
It is called: "Imagine"
Imagine seeing Him who creates flowers
Imagine being with Him who created the world
Imagine seeing the beauty of God the Father
Imagine Jesus stepping out to greet me
Imagine all of your ancestors calling to say hello
Imagine grandma's eyes
Imagine my surprise
Imagine meeting grandpa for the first time
Imagine time no more
Imagine majesty beyond belief
Imagine seeing His face
Imagine life with beauty so incredible that it dazzles your eyes
Imagine life with friends of all the ages
Imagine the God larger than the universe
Imagine me trying to put my arms around Him
Imagine me among the Angels
Imagine the wine of the Angels
Imagine lucky me
Imagine being among those who love you so
Imagine love without boundaries
Imagine light that warms
Imagine wind that is still
Imagine saying hello to the guardians of trust, hope and love
Imagine Him knowing your thoughts, your emotions, your needs
Imagine the delicacy of a rose
Imagine a guardian of beauty
Imagine Mary, the most beautiful mother in the universe
Imagine a rosary that glows with Mary's light
Imagine the love of Joseph
Imagine the tenderness of hands recreating the world each day
Imagine His life in each leaf, in each blade, in each person
Imagine being lifted and carried around Heaven by those who
        are powerful and swift
Imagine not one frightening thing
Imagine sitting with God to talk about what interests you
Imagine experiencing all of this simply because He loves us

Stages in Heaven - the original story

I walked, the other day, with a man who had been in Heaven for a long, long stay. He told me the following story.

"I began my journey in Heaven within the first stage," said he. "My life up to this event made me ready for the first step to the Stage of Ascent. I was happy and content, but I could not achieve the resounding joy of those who came to me from advanced stages I did not yet know. Though happy and content, I seemed to be drawn to move ahead. In fact, several folks came by to help me along."

"Through a variety of levels I passed until I was in a more beautiful setting of light, warmth, and knowledge. Again, I was drawn to move along. This time I heard folks sing a song of love, joy and delight. The urge to go forward with them was too strong to resist; we advanced to places I did not know could exist. Then, on an advanced stage, I heard music as I never heard before. I became a part of it and it re-sounded within me."

"A fellow of magnificent sound stood at some distance and called me along with a wave of an awe-inspiring wand. As I stepped forward, I caught the scent of Angels and flowers I had never noticed. A woman of light came up to me. Her scent was so joyous I lost sensual balance. Never had I experienced such a wonderful bouquet as this woman emitted from herself. The splendid flowers in her wake lifted their petals to certify her heavenly nature."

"I was quite content. Then, another glorious person stood before me holding a cup of the most beautiful sort. The cup was formed wholly of sublime light. 'Come with us,' said he. Then he turned, and I followed to a place glowing in the color of delicate rose. In this light, he lifted an earthen jar and poured a wine that embodied a blessed scent. Somehow, I knew there was nothing like this wine within my own memories. This earthen jar contained the scents of the earth as well as delicacies of the heavens."

"This fellow poured for each of us a full cup. Then, an Angel came with a platter of food delicious enough to put the least hungry person in the mood to dine. However, 'this is not enough,' said the man who led. 'We must have an orchestra and a floor for dancing. We must feel joy by the score. This is your destiny,'" said he.

"I thought I had been brought to the final Stage in Heaven. Then, one of glorious magnificence came into sight. I could not believe what I knew was true. This person was the Creator of the entire crew. I was in God's presence!"

"The fellow who led, in words of the mind, said, 'Only through the experience of marvelous events is one able to experience this magnificent sight.'"

"Within this stage of Heaven, I was given to realize that all previous happiness and joy was simply preparation for what I am experiencing. Now, after many stages of preparation, I am one with God."

Perhaps you too should listen to the stories brought to you in your journey. For, it is difficult to discern who it is that wants you to know the Glory of God. Listen, then, to the story told, for you may be talking to the messenger who wills to help you unfold the enchantments meant for your own life.

Stages in Heaven - Five Writings

Related Definitions:

Joy - the effects of the recognition that one is a part of the Spirit of Life.

Spirit of Life - the source of all positive energies.

Love - the Being of the Spirit of Life.

Person - individualized soul/body created and energized by Love.

Stages of Heaven – Places, or states of being, where one lives with the recognition and acceptance of one's own life-achievements in the relationship with Love.

Stages in Heaven - Five Writings

Stage One

I felt the release, then, the beginning of the journey. Turning to face into the light, I was drawn to the infinite. Yet, as the journey continued, I gained understanding of life in degrees of new consciousness.

Degrees 1-10
Physicality is remembered while it is being replaced with a broader awareness of life's purpose and events. Mother, Father, family and how life with them came to be; all these become clear. In addition, the reasons for life-lessons are given clarity.

Degrees 11-15
Here, we gain awareness of universes, galaxies, formations, as well as awareness of their energies.

Degrees 16-21
Definitions of energy variations are learned; including life-generation, health, growth, maturation, healing and recovery.

Degrees 22-36
Clarity comes about God's being; God's size, features, and inclusion. Discovered are - clarity about evolution, expansion, birth of human beings and Angels, formation of stars, clusters of energy with specific purposes, heat, radiation, definition, and the potential of creation.

Degrees 37-53
The transition is made from physicality to spirit. This transition leaves behind restrictions, limits, limiting definitions, doubts, and alignment with negative thoughts.

Degrees 54-86
We gain understanding that being without limits is achievable. We are awakened to the ability to seek help in releasing any restricting or limiting factor. We realize the potential of our own positive energies.

Degrees 87-91
Included is a broadening acceptance of the truth of these new dis-
coveries. The transitional pace slows to allow absorption of experiences; those that bolster the acceptance of perfection; the
acceptance of love that allows and /encourages expansion of
being, awareness, knowledge, universal commonness of creation
and creative energy.

Degree 92-96
Wonderment, experience, hearing encouraging voice(s), progress,
forward movement, exhilaration, acceptance of intuitive insights,
tasting - feeling - knowing the delicacy of goodness; complete
goodness.

Degree 97-99
Experience joy in the acceptance of goodness. Willing to be in
this place (state of being), on this stage of loving performance.

Degree 100
Contentment. Stepping out to do the pleasing thing. Participating
in events that fill one with pleasure. Creating and returning pleas-
urable events. Touching, healing, and helping others release their
own negative memories. In addition, accepting the full dimension
of creative love.

Resting and awash in the energy of acceptance, the realization of
wholeness, the knowledge of self as a part of the greater universe
that is ever expanding.

Stages in Heaven - Five Writings

Stage Two

Light is the guide on this stage; the light that is present in the plentiful group of those beings who love you. Light shapes and withdraws; attracts, then warms and cools in its guidance. This light is given with full confidence that you will flow with its nuances.

In degrees of understanding, one advances to the new stage of enhanced life performances. Joy is the motivator, only joy. Each vibration of the soul becomes saturated with joy.

All events (performances) are simply the expression of joy. Remembered things are performed in, and with, absolute joy. These include dance, song, game playing, storytelling, rituals of worship. Reaching out to touch others enriches joy in the heart. Each smile enriches the joy within others.

The games of life are played with recognition that each is an expression of God's gifts. It is clearly known that living experiences are expressions of those gifts. They enhance the development of the soul.

The recognition of another soul/person brings two types of joy. The first is simply the presence of the other person/soul. The second is the recognition that joy is without limits. Joy profoundly increases with the knowledge that a friend is present and joy-filled.

Limits of one's own thinking are recognized, then dissolved in the light of new realizations and new knowledge. Some limits disintegrate through the helpful light of other souls; some through one's own choice and willing. Always, the soul is filled with joy. The potential existing for more joy is without limits.

Joy is the motivator of all events. Joy motivates exploration and new awareness, thereby, dissolving of self-limitations. This joy brings absolute confidence that you are with God.

Stages in Heaven - Five Writings

Stage Three

Simplicity within chaos becomes known. The elements of creation are clearly known, i.e. Chemistry, Formation, Combinations, Attraction, Repulsion, Movement, and Purpose, among many others.

Reasons that the Spirit of Life created the universe become understood within each soul's being. Events, learning, and understanding are achieved both intellectually and intuitively.

A shouting voice, a song well sung, a story of simple love, a child's happiness, a mother's warm touch, a man's contribution, an angel's appearance, the richness of a simple act - all of these contribute to understanding the elements of creation.

An observation, a flower opening, the re-birth of grass, an insect that flies, a worm that digs, a dog barking, a pig oinking, crops growing, mountain scenes, a lake flowing, the extension of a helping hand, a healing touch - all of these are contributors to one's understanding of creation.

Intellectual pursuit, joining together, praising the Spirit of Life, announcing happiness, contributing to another's journey, sparking a flame of love, igniting a positive thought, standing on a precipice while viewing the infinite - each of these is an event helping in the explanation of the elements of creation.

In a mode of acceptance and relaxation, one is given an insight within each life-event. Each event is an adventure into understanding the universal elements.

Stage three is preparation for comprehending chaos and knowing how to influence its activities. Participation is essential in the process of gaining the insights required to understand universal elements. Insights and understanding are gifts of the Creator.

Stages in Heaven - Five Writings

Stage Four

On this stage, within this state of grace, one is performing and experiencing life events in a public circumstance. The realization that nothing is hidden is in its full dimension. All is known and known to be so. All events are honest, open, and are completed in full contentment.

Here, one observes as another soul prepares a star for its birthing. A second is observed in apprenticeship for the creation of a cathedral of light. A third is observed in full creative effort with Angels as they expand the universe. Here, one encounters Angels who remember the rules for creating distance, gravity, relativity, orbiting, heat, cooling, soil development, construction of seedlings, contents of air and water, hydro-construction and shaping of landscapes, the shaping of spheres, and the creation of mankind.

One man, gifted with the understanding of the construction of a flower, can be seen experimenting with the resilience of its skin, its frequency modulation and their interactions, while he prepares a formula for a hybrid flower never before conceived.

A woman of great vision sits in a chair made of creation-light and visualizes a mountain stream in the setting made of visible atoms. These atoms can be studied as a model for architects of systems that hydrate plants, give birth to fish and serve as a coolant for atmospheric heat. Another, walking high on a mountain of discarded creations, develops a formula for reinventing dreams and revitalizing healthy thought processes. A pair of practical researchers create positive energy from negative thoughts. This energy is to be used by those returning to earlier stages of Heaven to assist in the enlightenment of all.

A child, in the midst of a group, discovers the multipliers of the energy in groups of living things and beings. A culinary artist rediscovers an ancient formula that makes food taste as its consumer would most enjoy it. One person studies the habits of children in earlier stages of Heaven while fully confident of her ability to create a system for awakening them to the ecstasy existing in this more advanced stage, the fourth stage.

One person develops the propellant to push a star into its orbit. Another places a microscopic listening device in the center of a planet to allow future adventurers to study its unique qualities.

An Angel is observed while enlightening a person who seeks direction within his ecstatic wonderment. Many folks arrive at this stage in wonderment even though they have been happy and joyful within their explorations and learning events in previous stages.

Ecstasy has its source in the realized closeness to God, the Creator. The vibrations of the individual soul have become attuned to the presence of the Creative Being. This presence is in the forms of color, light, sound, frequency, movement, scents, warmth, and reactions to being loved without limit. Ecstasy is also caused by the Creator's actions. The actions of the Creator promote laughter and sharing.

One person is observed creating a process to deepen our understanding of love and the sympathetic vibrations it creates. Other folks rearrange galaxies, create music from gravitational pull, reduce a sea into a portable drop of water to be carried on the tip of a finger to a place being created for joyful events; like picnics, dancing and celebrating the gifts of life. One couple transforms a single grain into infinite varieties of foods for such celebrations.

A group of folks creates methods to communicate with people of Earth about the ecstasy birthed in loving one and other.

Equivalency, positive thought, creative effort, implementation of systems to increase love, the expansion of the universe, the perfection of human healing processes, and the intermingling of a variety of good spirits, are centers of activity in this Stage Four.

The presence of one person creates ecstasy in another. All events on this stage are preparation for the acceptance of Perfect Love; being completely synchronous with God, the Spirit of Life.

Note: written here is only a sampling of the attractions of progressive behavior on these stages of eternal life.

One objective of these writings is to stimulate the inquiry into perfection and the activities involved in perfecting while using the God-given gifts that bring one to perfection.

Stages in Heaven - Five Writings

Stage Five

Stage five is perfection. From stage four, in which one develops absolute confidence that he/she is a participant in the universal creation process, one progresses in the pathway of accepting Perfect Love.

With absolute confidence in one's own role in creation, one travels through perfecting light systems that change the frequency of the person's own light. This journey is begun only in absolute confidence. With absolute confidence that one is a part of the energies of universal creation, one easily accepts the transitions induced by the creator and source of energies.

This journey includes -

The revision of genetics that have been influenced within human life experiences; including those experiences of one's ancestors back to Adam and Eve.

Realignment of the soul's energy vibrations until each vibration attunes to God, its source.

Realignment of the purpose of individual life; life inside the energies of the Spirit of Life.

Being given images of Perfect Love to enable one to desire and envision one's self as a fully compatible part of such love.

Willingness to become a perfected individual energy within the universal set of perfect energies.

This journey is thrilling. It occurs in a motivational setting that allows, and superbly encourages, one to desire, will, act, and progress to the origin of perfect love. Changes in one's soul-light frequencies bring exhilaration and increased energy. This creates more desire and strengthening of the will to move forward and progress in closeness to God.

One knows of one's own perfecting through a variety of feedback systems including other individual beings. One is kept fully informed of progress in one's perfecting. This happens through music, familiar and motivating sounds, delightful images, and scents discovered on previous heavenly stages, as well as on Earth. Assurance of progress is absolute.

Persons, Angels, and other perfected beings visit the journeyer and listen to the journeyer's expression of personal experiences. They also exchange experiences through the sharing of marvelous stories of progress. Encouragement is always positive.

On this fifth stage of heaven, one journeyer experiences personal attunement with God as does a chime vibrating to the stroke of a perfect hammer. One senses, in every vibration of her/his soul, the scent of perfect being. One feels the presence of the Spirit of Life within self. One is encouraged to progress by observing an image of the interchange of love induced by a word, a song, and a touch.

One journeyer perceives the atoms of fiery light that move between each being in the perfected state. One hears a choir intoning the praise of God and discovers his own talents not revealed on previous stages of life.

Within this journey on stage five, a soul may ignite, explode beyond former boundaries, and re-form as a more magnificently attractive soul. One person pauses to create a new visual image of the Source and leaves it as an encouraging marker for other journeyers. This journeyer learns of perfection through the act of preparing lessons for others.

A soul may sense a further calling through creatures of different constitutions; animals, historic art characters, story collectors and other creations of human and Angel imaginations. One assimilates images of perfect beings and, while searching those images, finds they are real and capable of discussing the perfecting process while emitting perfect energies of love.

Each journeyer is unique. Each pathway to perfection is full of options. Each option is a motivational part of the perfecting journey. All options are created by the Source of life energies. The journeyer will enjoy rich experiences to share when the fullness of one's meeting with God occurs.

In the state of Perfection, after the journey within pure love, one converses freely with God. The Creator encourages the telling of life stories and the sharing of experiences related to each story. The telling of these stories produces endless delight, contagious happiness, joy, ecstasy, and oneness of all beings with the Creator.

Within these stories, creation also happens. As one tells of a life event or experience, one also creates improved conditions for humankind. The act of reviewing events of progress in one's own life creates increasingly positive environmental settings for those within their own journey to know Perfect Love.

Imagining, recollecting and sharing happy, joyous, and ecstatic experiences create an ever-expanding enlightenment of all beings in their own journey of individualization and progress to perfection.

Those who live in the perfected state-of-being collaborate with the Creator in perfect love while expanding love through their own living and recalling of life events.

BOOK FOUR:

Angels

Twenty-Three Stories,
Meditations and Spiritual Exercises

Angels

Index of Stories and Exercises

Stories written as though they had been told to me.

*If a story seems beyond your imagination,
return to it and study the meanings of a word or sentence.
Let repeated readings of the story expand your imagination,
as well as the positive thoughts and images you hold.*

February 27, 2006

As the human mind opens to the value and intent of Angels, the possibilities of study and learning through events are without limit. Obviously so. Angels are given birth within Perfect Love, Perfect Love that is always perfect. As humans are given life from the depths of the Spirit of Life, so are Angels. Angels are individualized from within the energies of Source.

In birth, an Angel is also given full awareness of the Source-Angel relationship. In its birthing an Angel is imbued with emotional and mental knowledge of being perfectly loved.

An Angel's birth is directly of Source. Through willing, the Giver of Life creates the individual Angel. All energies of the Angel correspond directly and perfectly with the Source.

When a human soul encounters an Angel, the soul is also privileged to experience absolute confidence in the veracity of the Angel's being. This gift is innate in the Angel's being.

An Angel is birthed as a simple individualized Being of Source; an extension of Source, loved and sustained by Source.

Spiritual exercise:

Sit or lie in your favorite place. Relax. Take in three deep breaths. Close your eyes. Count back from five down to zero. Each number will take you deeper into relaxation. At three, you will feel more relaxed. When you get to zero you will feel the tension leaving your body. Stay still for a moment and let go of all tension.

Visualize or imagine being in a beautiful place. See the details of trees, color, contour, texture, fabric, the coolness, or warmth. In this place is a beautiful door. Above the door is a sign that says, "Source of Love." Walk to the door and open it. Go into the room and find a comfortable place to be.

Now, in this comfortable place, let your imagination take command. Imagine or visualize the following event.

• Imagine an Angel walking up to you in this beautiful place. Listen as the Angel tells you about being part of Perfect Love.

February 28, 2006

Understanding the life of an Angel requires one to move out of the realm of the human frame of reference, which includes negative thoughts.

So, let us visualize or imagine we are now in the realm of perfect love. Visualize or imagine this: feel the touch of all-present love on your skin as you feel a breeze. Let your cells become saturated with the perfection of this love. As you do so, life now is like that of an Angel. An Angel's thoughts are of perfection in Source.

As an Angel visualizes or imagines perfection in a human being, so the human becomes. However, a human must will to have the perfection, and act to gain it.

Spiritual exercise:

Sit or lie in your favorite place. Relax. Take in three deep breaths. Close your eyes. Count back from five down to zero. Each number will take you deeper into relaxation. At three, you will feel more relaxed. When you get to zero you will feel the tension leaving your body. Stay still for a moment and let go of all tension.

Visualize or imagine being in a beautiful place. See the details of trees, color, contour, texture, fabric, the coolness, or warmth. In this place is a beautiful door. Above the door is a sign that says, "Angels' Gathering Place." Walk to the door and open it. Go into the room and find a comfortable place to be.

Now, in this comfortable place, let your imagination take command. Imagine or visualize any of the following events occurring as the Angels greet one and then the other Angel.

1. Imagine each Angel recognizing another's Angelic scent.

2. Imagine each Angel acknowledging the ecstasy contained within each other.

3. Imagine the Angels acknowledging each other as a simple part of Source. Simple, meaning unchanged from Source; as created; containing only energies of Source.

4. Imagine sparks of Perfect Love igniting as the Angels speak.

5. Imagine Angels letting the Divine Light flow to each other Angel.

6. Imagine Angels discussing new thoughts of how to serve the Creator.

7. Imagine Angels in conversation about perpetuating positive thoughts.

8. Notice how you are attracted to the positive energies of the Angels.

March 1, 2006

Intent and purpose are the same for an Angel. An Angel with the intent to promote good health promotes the achievement of good health in all beings and things intended to receive it.

Spiritual exercise:

Sit or lie in your favorite place. Relax. Take in three deep breaths.

Close your eyes. Count back from five down to zero. Each number will take you deeper into relaxation. At three, you will feel more relaxed. When you get to zero you will feel the tension leaving your body. Stay still for a moment and let go of all tension.

Visualize or imagine being in a beautiful place. See the details of trees, color, contour, texture, fabric, the coolness, or warmth. In this place is a beautiful door. Above the door is a sign that says, "Angel Interventions." Walk to the door and open it. Go into the room and find a comfortable place to be.

Now, in this comfortable place, let your imagination take command. Imagine or visualize any of the following acts of Angelic kindness.

1. Imagine Angels creating a place where healing thoughts are given to those who need healing.

2. Imagine Angels helping researchers find the cure for cancer.

3. Imagine Angels forming a pool of cool water for desert travelers.

4. Imagine Angels transmitting a light that brightens the day of people.

5. Imagine Angels creating a fruit so packed with nourishment that it would quickly revive and refresh a starving person.

6. Imagine your Guardian Angel helping you to release negative memories. Give permission for the healing light of the Angel to flow through you causing all of your cells to function in health.

6. Imagine Angels enabling a person to speak in each language of worldly listeners.

March 2, 2006

Telling you about storms of the Universe is fun for me. Being in the midst of a "universal blow" is like being a part of a high-powered thunderstorm. The sounds are incredibly fascinating. They rattle every vibration of your soul. They leave not a chance for negative energy to survive. The universe cleanses itself of energies left over after creation and restoration activities. All energies are reoriented to perfection, the perfection of the Creator.

I was present and near Earth during a sunspot eruption. There is no anticipation of such storms. One simply experiences the eruption of energies while feeling great joy in being within this universal happening.

Wow! This expression comes quickly to mind when you experience the approaching burst of light, heat, pressure, and hues of color. When these energies pass through you, the feeling is similar to being born. Patterns of energies are disrupted, refreshed, and then settled into perfect affiliation.

Light fills your thoughts enlightening your view of your life. Awareness develops about the history of humanity, the reality of other created life, and life systems. Sound re-attunes you to Source's presence. Within you, the sound resonates each of your own vibrations. Each of your own vibrations is attuned to one sound that is native to the Creator.

You can fully experience the joy of one sound inherent within the Creator. This one sound is so joyful that it could sustain eternal celebration. The next wave of energy from the wide-ranging storm expands the potential of the person who desires, wills, and acts to create additional goodness.

The scent of this cleansing energy is something like fresh air blowing down a mountain and over an earthly forest of trees and flowers. The soul is massaged in the light and sound waves. It is as though the hands of Source were touching your skin transmitting happiness and ecstasy to every sensitive vibration within you.

There are parallel experiences on earth that can be experienced when a person is open to accepting such experiences.

Spiritual exercise:

Sit or lie in your favorite place. Relax. Take in three deep breaths.

Close your eyes. Count back from five down to zero. Each number will take you deeper into relaxation. At three, you will feel more relaxed. When you get to zero you will feel the tension leaving your body. Stay still for a moment and let go of all tension.

Visualize or imagine being in a beautiful place. See the details of trees, color, contour, texture, fabric, the coolness, or warmth. In this place is a beautiful door. Above the door is a sign that says, "Ecstatic Experiences." Walk to the door and open it. Go into the room and find a comfortable place to be.

Now, in this comfortable place, let your imagination take command. Imagine or visualize any of the following events.

1. Imagine your skin becoming sensitive to the touch of the wind.

2. Imagine releasing the limits of your view of life.

3. Imagine the scent of one you love. Let that scent fill your mind.

4. Imagine your fingertips fully experiencing the delicacy of a flower.

5. Imagine letting go of self-protection; letting Source be present to you.

6. Imagine the noise of a thunderclap vibrating each cell of your body.

7. Imagine the changing light created by the sun on a mountainside.

8. Imagine the sound of a bull's tongue lapping the water's surface after a dry spell.

March 2, 2006

Awakening has many meanings. One can awaken to a deeper understanding of familiar things, or be awakened to the unknown.

Angels intend to awaken human folks to the more complete universe in which we live. A tap on the shoulder that is felt physically is an occasional method of awakening. A hug that warms a cold emotional state is one method. The appearance of a lost object in an unsuspected place is a fun method of awakening a person. Many awakenings are small happenings with minor surprises. The measurement of success of an awakening is the effect it has on the person being awakened.

A simple awakening experience offers an abundance of knowledge and feelings that wait just beyond the awakening. The result of the awakening is dependent upon the person's desire, as well as the willingness to progress by taking action.

An example - a woman was bored with a lasting feeling that she was a victim of circumstances. Boredom readied her for an awakening. Her Angel touched her shoulder. She turned in response and saw her self-reflection in a window. Her image lacked signs of energy, happiness, and contentment. The desire to experience the exhilaration of achievement burst forth in her mind. Then, she willed to be excited about her contributions made through her work. She raised the muscles of her face into a smile. In her reflection, she now saw the hint of happiness and she realized that being fulfilled was a decision she had to make.

Deciding to be fulfilled through her own contributions, she examined her activities while accepting the accomplishments within each. Someone passed by her, she smiled and the radiance of the other's returned smile filled her heart. She congratulated a friend on her accomplishment and saw her friend's face ignite in smiling response. She lifted her face to Source and said, "Thanks for the opportunity to contribute through my talents and skills developed over years of practice."

Work became pleasure. Accomplishment became purpose. Achievement became intent translated into activity. Activity produced satisfying results. Purpose created a flow of positive energy. This positive energy satisfied her as well as the receiver of her contribution to the positive flow of life giving energies.

Spiritual exercise:

Sit or lie in your favorite place. Relax. Take in three deep breaths.

Close your eyes. Count back from five down to zero. Each number will take you deeper into relaxation. At three, you will feel more relaxed. When you get to zero you will feel the tension leaving your body. Stay still for a moment and let go of all tension.

Visualize or imagine being in a beautiful place. See the details of trees, color, contour, texture, fabric, the coolness, or warmth. In this place is a beautiful door. Above the door is a sign that says, "Awakenings." Walk to the door and open it. Go into the room and find a comfortable place to be.

Now, in this comfortable place, let your imagination take command. Imagine or visualize any of the following events.

1. Imagine an Angel touching your shoulder and awakening you to the many good things you have done in your lifetime. Imagine listing these good things.

2. Imagine an Angel appearing to you. Give permission for the Angel's light to awaken you to the things you enjoy about your work. Things like your contributions to meeting goals, helping customers, helping other employees achieve their objectives, organization, quality, creating new items, solving important problems, stimulating awareness, etc.

3. Imagine an Angel reciting the names of people who need you; parents, children, colleagues, customers, people in need and people who achieve because of your contribution to their efforts.

March 2, 2006

Magnificent love is also expressed as sound. Those sounds include a note played on the piano. Properly heard, this sound can be as thrilling as the sound of a full orchestra. The level of quality heard in a tone, a note, or a frequency within a note depends upon the breadth of thinking of the listener.

If the vibrating sound is interpreted as noise, only the ear will hear it. However, suppose a person is gifted to know the vibrations of the universe and has discovered that each vibration is perfectly in tune with all other vibrations. With this enlightened view, one is enabled to hear and enjoy even the briefest vibration and know its importance to universal harmony.

An example - John, in wonderment about the essential elements of the Universe, desired to learn of those elements. He willed to investigate and traveled to his first instructive session. The opening of his mind brought ample Angelic assistance and abundantly increased his learning abilities.

His curiosity increased. His mind focused on the experience of the effects that sounds created within him. These sounds were varied according to the formula of associated light, spiritual intent, and ultimate use. John experimented until he experienced many sounds that set off ecstasy within him. In this accomplishment, he realized he could hear the smallest sound. Consequently, any sound created by Source, no matter its dimension, set John into complete attunement to the nature of Source.

Spiritual exercise:

Sit or lie in your favorite place. Relax. Take in three deep breaths.

Close your eyes. Count back from five down to zero. Each number will take you deeper into relaxation. At three, you will feel more relaxed. When you get to zero you will feel the tension leaving your body. Stay still for a moment and let go of all tension.

Visualize or imagine being in a beautiful place. See the details of trees, color, contour, texture, fabric, the coolness, or warmth. In this place is a beautiful door. Above the door is a sign that says, "Awareness of Sounds." Walk to the door and open it. Go into the room and find a comfortable place to be.

Now, in this comfortable place, let your imagination take command. Imagine or visualize the following event.

• Visualize or imagine an Angel standing near you. Imagine the Angel sending out a sound that pleases you. As the sound flows from the Angel, allow your mind to listen to that sound. Enjoy and remember the feelings associated with the sound of this Angel. Imagine hearing this sound anytime the Angel is nearby.

March 3, 2006

Spartan conditions can open a person's awareness to the existence of surrounding beauty. Some artists are gifted observers of the details of life's existence. Others must learn such observation skills.

To be capable of reproducing the reality and images of life, a person must notice - color, shape, intensity, fabric construction, hues, integration of parts, appearance of the whole. The person must also notice source, structure, roundness, edges, sharpness, clarity, impressions created, strictness of interpretation, fullness of the artist's stroke; also the depth of color or its shallowness, blend of pieces, originality of construction, temperature implied, distance intended, weight implied, mood implied, and interpretations of legacy.

For an Angel such creative art is a flow-through endeavor. When an Angel intends that beauty surround you, the Angel's thoughts create the scene. Imagine this, in a situation of isolation a person desires to be in a place of beauty, soothing sound, and refreshing breeze. Empathetic to this need, the Angel creates the place desired simply by thinking of it.

Spiritual exercise:

Sit or lie in your favorite place. Relax. Take in three deep breaths.

Close your eyes. Count back from five down to zero. Each number will take you deeper into relaxation. At three, you will feel more relaxed. When you get to zero you will feel the tension leaving your body. Stay still for a moment and let go of all tension.

Visualize or imagine being in a beautiful place. See the details of trees, color, contour, texture, fabric, the coolness, or warmth. In this place is a beautiful door. Above the door is a sign that says,

"Mentoring Angels." Walk to the door and open it. Go into the room and find a comfortable place to be.

Now, in this comfortable place, let your imagination take command. Imagine or visualize any of the following events.

• Visualize or imagine a piece of art that you would like to create. Imagine an Angel coming over to you, touching you, and telling you how to begin creating the art piece. Imagine the Angel continuing to tell you what to do. Imagine hearing the voice of the Angel within you.

• If you are a gifted artist, imagine the Angel giving you a subtle interpretation of what you are creating, thus bringing about dimensions that others cannot conceive.

• If you are a casual observer of surroundings, imagine the Angel focusing your view to minute detail and intricate observations.

March 3, 2006

Thoughts set perceived limits. Limiting thoughts set the boundaries of one's awareness and capabilities.

The light flowing through an Angel is capable of locating and exposing a limiting thought.

Spiritual exercise:

Sit or lie in your favorite place. Relax. Take in three deep breaths.

Close your eyes. Count back from five down to zero. Each number will take you deeper into relaxation. At three, you will feel more relaxed. When you get to zero you will feel the tension leaving your body. Stay still for a moment and let go of all tension.

Visualize or imagine being in a beautiful place. See the details of trees, color, contour, texture, fabric, the coolness, or warmth. In this place is a beautiful door. Above the door is a sign that says, "Extending Your Limits." Walk to the door and open it. Go into the room and find a comfortable place to be.

Now, in this comfortable place, let your imagination take command. Imagine or visualize any of the following events.

• Visualize or imagine an Angel touching you with the intent of extending your thinking to new dimensions of realization and enlightenment.

Relax deeply and say, "Angel of goodness, touch me with the purpose of identifying my restricting thoughts about …………"

"Also, please give me the insights I need to live life well."

• Imagine the light of the Angel flowing through you. Imagine this light flowing down, through your head, your chest, your stomach, your hips, and down through your toes. Allow the light to go to the places within you to release thoughts and memories that restrict your thinking about the subject you selected.

Imagine new, more expansive thoughts coming into your mind. Remember these thoughts. Handwrite these thoughts for reference.

ANGELIC PERFORMANCES

We call it dancing. However, for Angels, it is more like floating in synchronous rhythm with universal music. Angels feel the rhythm of universal chaos as they gather to enjoy the celebration requested by the Creator. They float with the musical sound waves created by chaotic existence. Seem like fun to you?

Imagine having the absolute confidence that the chaos of the Universe will take you on a wide, universal swing and return you, with your partner, to the dance floor where you began this dance. Allow yourself to accept the idea that chaos always knows who you are, where you are, and where you desire to be. Imagine trusting at such a high level that you let go of all perceived control and let chaos take you to a destiny of fun, thrills of the unknown, and assurance that you are a guiding part of chaos itself.

Imagine yourself saying to your partner, "come with me to a place we don't know via a route yet uncreated while we enjoy complete trust in the music that carries us." Know that it is possible for you to witness the dance-of-the-Angels as they celebrate Source's being and their own contributions to universal existence in Perfect Love. When you allow yourself to observe this dance of universal joy, you will note the cycles of light influenced by each set of dancing Angels. Light of infinite hues rearranges itself to match the uniqueness created within the movement of the individual Angel.

You will note the gravitational pull as it follows a grouping of Angelic dancers who are always in rhythm with the chaotic flow of energy of the Galaxy, the Universe. Also, note the feeling of silent movement as the waves of energy pour from around the dancing sets. What you observe is a creation designed to please your intellect, your emotions. It is designed to confirm your beliefs in the power of love and serve your desire for overwhelmingly positive companionship.

Yet, you contribute to this universal celebration, this dance with chaotic energy; this movement within perennial universal refreshment. As an observer, you create pleasure for the performers. As a person progressing to the acceptance of Perfect Love, you absorb confidence from those who contain absolute confidence and absolute knowledge. Within your own observation, you become one influenced by the teachers who are motivated by your progress and gratified in contributing to your awakenings.

March 5, 2006

Mother was concerned for her child and discovered a method to help him know right choices. She gave him memories of good and bad choices. Good choices brought happiness. Bad choices always brought a feeling of loneliness and isolation.

The child learned that happiness and joy are results of choosing positive actions. A smile brings human touch. A word of thanks brings a warm smile of acceptance.

Though the guidance of an Angel is similar, there is a difference. That difference being the method of transmitting the message. Angels have the power to impress thoughts, that is, to bring thoughts into your consciousness. Though Angels do appear in physical form to offer assistance, a more common way is thought-impression. Knowing the person's history provides an Angel alternative ways to impress thoughts into the person's mind.

It works like this - all thought is known to Angels. The source of thought is also known. The Angel also knows about methods of intervention and the value of timing those interventions. Respecting human free will, the Angel's option is to cause a choice to be considered. The person thinking about an action, or taking an action, is impressed with a thought of right-or-wrong, and good-or-bad consequences.

The responsibility of the Angel is to provide guidance within the use of free will. "Why the Angel's concern?" one might ask. Thought is a co-creator of the life-environment of all created beings living within the same plane of life. Action follows thought and is a co-creator of life-environment.

This truth can be understood through daily observations. A person observes that a series of negative thoughts generates an environment that lacks hope and charity. The same person can observe that a positive thought and action attract those of the same nature. One observes that positive thoughts, stories, and actions create an environment of hope, charity, happiness, joy, love, and creative effort.

Therefore, with this same knowledge, an Angel is aware that a "thought of positive guidance" has the potential to influence the environment of all people in all time.

Consider this - one Angel who influences one person to choose a positive thought, or take a positive action, has potentially influenced all of the future of humankind.

Contemplate this if you so desire - one thought of yours, either positive or negative, may influence all of humankind's future. If you wonder about this truth, you might consider answering the following questions.

1. Why are people attracted to others who fill themselves with positive thoughts, and lead others to positive thought?

2. Why are folks attracted to others who respect and love them?

3. Why are people attracted to others who believe themselves to be loveable?

4. Why have the stories about the Creator been so attracting to so many people throughout the history of humankind?

5. Why are the results of positive thinking and actions satisfying to so many people?

6. Why is peace the result of positive thoughts and actions?

March 5, 2006

"Who needs guidance?" one might ask. It is a matter of timing. Each person needs guidance within a lifetime. Angelic resources are super-ample to provide all guidance needed. However, people are destined to be self-guiding. The goal is to help each person achieve self-guidance.

The answer, then, is simple - the person needing guidance, direction, help, assistance, or support receives it according to the need.

Spiritual exercise:

Sit or lie in your favorite place. Relax. Take in three deep breaths.

Close your eyes. Count back from five down to zero. Each number will take you deeper into relaxation. At three, you will feel more relaxed. When you get to zero you will feel the tension leaving your body. Stay still for a moment and let go of all tension.

Visualize or imagine being in a beautiful place. See the details of trees, color, contour, texture, fabric, the coolness, or warmth. In this place is a beautiful door. Above the door is a sign that says, "Guidance for Those in Need." Walk to the door and open it. Go into the room and find a comfortable place to be.

Now, in this comfortable place, let your imagination take command.

• Imagine being with the Angel of great wisdom. Say to the Angel, "I need guidance to help me"

The guidance you need is provided. The provider of the guidance may be your inner voice; it might be the next person you meet; the provider may be someone you trust, or a stranger whom you happen to meet.

The objective is to open yourself to receive the guidance you need from the source selected to provide the guidance.

March 5, 2006

The best we can do is to bring peace. Within peace, Source permeates all.

The one who creates an armistice creates an opportunity to generate and extend love. Within peace, possibilities can be explored because current limiting thoughts can be discussed and changed. Within peace, it is possible to have trust. Having trust, one can be trusted.

Armistice brings the opportunity for mutual respect to develop into mutual assistance. Mutual assistance brings about mutual goals. Mutual goals motivate constructive acts. Constructive acts bring about shared love.

Armistice is a pathway needing continual cultivation in human life. The tools of this cultivation are love of Creator, love of creation, love of self, inner peace, positive thoughts, openness to positive guidance, and good example. Another useful tool is the knowledge that other people affect your own progress.

March 5, 2006

Awakening in the darkness - expecting darkness to prevail, I was flooded with light. This was not what I expected. "Why is this light present within my gloomy mood?" I wondered. "Why, when my children would soon know of my passing, is this night experience illuminated?"

Yet, I recognized the light. I had experienced it on other occasions though never accepting it or allowing its influence. "Persistent, aren't you?" came the response to my questions, loud and clear in my ear.

"Your view must be different than mine since you ask such a silly question," I retorted. "Not of necessity, but certainly true," came the responding answer. "Do you have children?" I questioned. "No, I do not." "Then how can your understanding of my situation contain an ounce of veracity?" was my response.

"If forced to talk about this subject of my dying, I would like to talk with someone who has the experience to be empathetic," I blurted out into the light that now began to permeate my soul. Not one additional word was spoken. The entire experience was gentle, of love, and it saturated my complete being. Nor did I protest.

No claim of veracity was made. No protest of my rash behavior was uttered. No claim of superior knowledge was stated. No mention was made about superior information of the pathway to acceptance. No indication was given about my own misunderstanding. My life's current direction was not mentioned. No recollection of past errors was described. Not one negative or reductive thought was transmitted.

There was only the light, present and welcoming, absorbed by me. I was satiated, then the flow to me ceased. I was fulfilled. I comprehended the end of Earth-life for me. I had accepted the event and I was peace-filled.

HONORING AN ANGEL

March 6, 2006

"How do you keep an Angel happy?" you asked.

Well, an Angel's contentment does have something to do with you. The realm of the difference you make for an Angel is in your progress toward unity with Source; and an occasional word of thanks, of course.

You may recall that a purpose of an Angel is to be of help to you individually, and to all of humankind. You may recall that one of the historically persistent reasons for prayer is to honor Source and offer thanksgiving. You recall that a person who says "thank you" does brighten your feelings.

One simple and effective way to honor the Angel(s) helping you is to say, or think, this: "I appreciate you. I appreciate your help in my life. Thank you."

March 6, 2006

An event of major importance to one who is created to assist other beings, and dedicated to that destiny, is - observable progress of the assisted person.

Imagine coaching a child in how to kick a ball to a goal. Recall the importance of that achievement to the child as well as to you. Imagine helping a person reach a lifetime goal. Imagine the joy of the achievement for one who is now capable of credible contributions after months of study and practice.

Spiritual exercise:

Sit or lie in your favorite place. Relax. Take in three deep breaths.

Close your eyes. Count back from five down to zero. Each number will take you deeper into relaxation. At three, you will feel more relaxed. When you get to zero you will feel the tension leaving your body. Stay still for a moment and let go of all tension.

Visualize or imagine being in a beautiful place. See the details of trees, color, contour, texture, fabric, the coolness, or warmth. In this place is a beautiful door. Above the door is a sign that says, "Mutual Healing." Walk to the door and open it. Go into the room and find a comfortable place to be.

Now, in this comfortable place, let your imagination take command. Imagine or visualize any of the following events.

1. Imagine knowing the destiny of a reluctant child and awakening him to progressive understanding of who he is and to his full potential. Imagine and write the value of this achievement to the child and to you, the awakener.

2. Imagine you are the person whose life style positively affects one who is searching for inner peace.

3. Imagine developing a lesson plan for a currently unmotivated student. Imagine the lessons igniting the child's desire to learn.

4. Suppose an adult had lost confidence about being loveable. Imagine you are gifted to know the right words to say, and the proper timing to speak those words to this person. Imagine that your words cause the change of the person's thinking and stimulate the person to regain full confidence.

5. An Angel is created with a purpose, a destiny. You and each person of history and those of the future are a part of an Angel's destiny. Imagine now, an Angel is standing nearby to help you.

March 7, 2006

Timing, as is frequently said, is important.

Since Angels know the existence of thought, and thought's source, the factor of timing becomes important. Timing is a challenge, a decision left to the Angel. Making an accurate decision requires skill. It may be comforting for you to know that Infinite Love does not give up when an action taken is unsuccessful.

An Angel learns. Nuances are important in such learning. Examples of nuances that affect the timing of intervention:

- Is the person ready to receive a message of encouragement?

- Should the important message be received only in a state of health?

- Within any day of feeling elated, will the person hear the inner-voice?

Urgency of the message to be delivered is another consideration. Suppose the message would make the difference between continued health and catastrophe? Considering these challenges might help a person realize the active involvement of an Angel in one's own life events.

Spiritual Exercise:

Think about and list what you must do to prepare to communicate with an Angel and hear the Angel's messages.

Relax.

State your need.

1.   4.

2.   5.

3.   6.

March 6, 2006

As a part of Source, does an Angel have to choose a direction to take? An intellectual challenge about what direction to take and the choices to make in life create excitement. The challenge of being involved in problem solving and progressive movement to Perfect Love is also exciting.

Choices abound for an Angel. Possession of full knowledge does not eliminate choice. Think of it this way - as a unique being, an Angel discovers that the Creator has provided a bundle of choices for achieving a goal. An Angel might select to speak in parables or tell stories without interpretation, or appear in physical form to impress a person or a selected group.

An Angel might choose to whisper in an ear, attract the eye, touch a shoulder, write a poem, speak through a trusted person, find an important lost article, directly impress a thought, expand an image, or cause a painting to cry.

An Angel might cause responsive movement to or away from an object, change the effects of gravity, open another's mind to your spoken word, send a messenger, let light flow through another person's hand, or create direct communications from a healing practitioner.

Or, an Angel might impress your need in another's mind, change the taste of food or drink, cause the recognition of the damage inflicted by a habit, start a refrain of prayer, lift your spirit through the sound of another person's voice, encourage you through a lovely vision, bring beauty into your perception, or record your own acts of charity.

An angel might whisper "I love you" when you are in an empty room, mark a sign with a familiar symbol, trace the source of a pleasant thought, bring you to one who truly loves you, show a sign of another's concern, peak your perception of a good experience, or release the tension of a threatening situation.

An Angel could raise a hand in witness to your goodness, encourage a friend to accept your love, sing a song through your voice, speak a message through your mind, or allow your entry through a closed door. An Angel might bring you through an impossible journey, touch and cure a major disease, extend your hand to one in need even though you are tired, or speak, through your voice, to one who is lonely.

Ah yes, these and many more choices are available within the created bundle of choices.

March 7, 2006

Participation in life activities is a stimulant. Participation causes the desire to achieve one's created potential.

Each creature is destined to contribute to its environment, its society, and those with whom it shares life. Each creature contains a natural urge to contribute to the well-being of others. Each, in its basic nature, wants to contribute to others in the process of living-life-well.

The same is true for Angels. Participation in creation, re-creation, refreshment of life and the living of it, as well as progress towards unity, is essential to an Angel's being.

How does one help an Angel participate in one's own life? It is a matter of asking, listening, and developing your skill in being aware of, and discerning the value of the message; also discerning who is providing the help you request.

Spiritual exercise:

Sit or lie in your favorite place. Relax. Take in three deep breaths.

Close your eyes. Count back from five down to zero. Each number will take you deeper into relaxation. At three, you will feel more relaxed. When you get to zero you will feel the tension leaving your body. Stay still for a moment and let go of all tension.

Visualize or imagine being in a beautiful place. See the details of trees, color, contour, texture, fabric, the coolness, or warmth. In this place is a beautiful door. Above the door is a sign that says, "Seeking Angelic Help." Walk to the door and open it. Go into the room and find a comfortable place to be.

Now, in this comfortable place, let your imagination take command. Imagine or visualize an Angel in the room with you. Do the following-

• Ask the Angel to help in your planning for the day, the week, the year, an event, your career, your spiritual journey, etc.

• Stay quiet and listen for the response.

• Develop your skill of hearing the voice that speaks within you through repetition.

• Develop an awareness of external acts that awaken you. Those include comments made to you, a well-timed kindness, or an offer of aid.

• Develop the skill of discerning the quality of a message. Test the message intuitively and through your own personal experience.

• Learn to trust the good messages and take action based on these messages.

• Ask the Angel to visualize or imagine success for you in your future activities.

• Trust that the Angel's visualization has become truth.

• Act in confidence that the Angel has a need to help you and the ability to influence events in your life.

• Say "Thanks."

Note: developing the skill of listening to you "inner voice" may require the assistance of a Spiritual Director.

March 7, 2006

Energy is the essence of Creation. Source creates all energy. A person is capable of renaming a personally held energy and changing it from positive to negative. However, energies are created to be positive.

Any thought energy that has been changed to a negative energy is an un-comfortable one.

Each created entity recognizes positive energy. Examples are the flowers that grow in positive energy; animals flourish in positive energy; people are healthy and recover in positive energy.

An Angel is always positive energy with the intent and purpose of creating positive energies and re-transforming negative energies.

March 7, 2006

Eternity contains all thought. Thought is created by thinking beings. Suppose Source provides a storage place where rejected negative thoughts are captured. Suppose those negative thought energies await being re-transformed into positive energies.

Now, you have re-transformed, envisioned or imagined the possibility of one more purpose of Angels. That is, the transformation of rejected negative thought into positive energies. Each Angel contributes by visualizing or imagining Divine Light surrounding the captured negative thoughts. Surrounded by this angelic light, they absorb the transforming positive energy.

All thinking beings can contribute to the availability of positive energy that transforms negative thoughts. The process of involvement is simply to visualize or imagine the flow of Divine Light through you to the area that contains the negative thoughts. This allows the process of transformation to occur as established by the Creator. Angels will direct the Divine Light to the area containing the negative energies.

In the receipt of plentiful Divine Light, a negative thought is re-transformed into positive energy to again be a part of universal health.

Spiritual Exercise:

Schedule a time to sit quietly, relax, and allow Divine Light to flow through you. Visualize or imagine this light flowing through you as an Angel directs the light to the area where rejected negative thoughts are captured.

Assume that the light flowing through you has joined with the light of the Angels to provide re-transformation to those negative thoughts.

TIMING IN COMMUNICATING WITH AN ANGEL

March 7, 2006

Timing in communicating with an Angel is also up to you.

Angels are aware of thoughts.

Select the timing of communication with an Angel depending on conditions-

- Designate a special time each day or week to communicate with your Angel.

- In an emergency, communicate now.

- When you are preparing for a future event, take time to visualize or imagine an Angel's involvement with your success.

- In current events, visualize or imagine the help of an Angel while engaged in an event.

TURMOIL

March 7, 2006

Turmoil is a part of Creation. Renewal requires turmoil. Turmoil that renews is different from turmoil associated with human anxiety. Universal turmoil rearranges atoms for useful purposes. Anxious turmoil restricts progress. Angels know the difference.

The touch of an Angel, or a given awakening thought, can change anxiety by creating the understanding that turmoil is a universal tool used in creating refreshed and progressive existence and happiness in life.

Peace is here and there. The source of peace is Divinity. The possibility of having "peace within" also comes through Angels, people, animals, and other created beings. Why are there so many sources of "peace within?" Peace is the result of the presence of Divine love. So is Life Itself.

About the Author:

John Patrick Gatton, Biography

Patrick is a Master Mentor, Certified Hypnotherapist, and Practitioner of Healing Prayer. Teaching Creative Visualization, he guides clients to create new possibilities in healing. He specializes in facilitating the well-being of his clients while they adjust to increasing healing and its positive life-altering effects.

During his own experience of cancer, a friend offered healing prayer. This prayer was so powerfully helpful that Patrick later trained as a Healing Prayer Practitioner. Over the years, he has worked with hundreds of people who are living the experience of cancer using prayer and hypnotherapy to engage the principles of healing. Patrick understands the trauma that bad news brings, and the adjustments we can make in our lives to enable us live in wellbeing. He has been cancer-free for over seventeen years.

After the death of his 19-year-old daughter, Cynthia Jean, Patrick began to write inspirational poems and stories. The first poem was written the day-after Cynthia died and was titled "Imagine." The preamble of "Imagine" was, "Daddy, I am ecstatic. You must write my poem for my friends." The poem began with the phrase, "Imagine seeing Him Who creates flowers." The proven healing power of the words of this poem convinced him that he should share his experiences with those who are within their own journey of healing. "Imagine" has been read in churches across the country. It inspires healing in a variety of life experiences.

As a Healing Prayer Practitioner and Hypnotherapist, he brings uplifting messages and practical processes for healing to his clients. He trains Caretakers in how to help those in critical need. His workbook, "Healing, A Journey" provides Caretakers with a process to help those in keen need feel comfortable and confident that healing is possible. Healing can be a journey of great spiritual and personal growth when assisted and encouraged by proper guidance. The stories and meditation exercises contained in this book guide one to deeper understanding of how to heal and a deeper realization of being healed.

Patrick's Inspirational stories and poems stimulate positive physical, mental, emotional, and spiritual healing when we need it most.

To Order Copies of

A Journey with the Spirit of Life:

STORIES THAT INSPIRE AND ENHANCE HEALING

by John Patrick Gatton

I.S.B.N. 1-59879-516-3

Order Online at:
www.authorstobelievein.com

By Phone Toll Free at:
1-877-843-1007